ADHD, SO WHAT?

TURN YOUR DIAGNOSIS INTO YOUR DESTINY

JORDAN GHEE

MYND
MATTERS

To purchase books in bulk, please contact the publisher.

Mynd Matters Publishing
2690 Cobb Parkway SE
Ste A5-375
Smyrna, GA 30080

www.myndmatterspublishing.com

ISBN: 978-1-963874-76-1 (pbk)
ISBN: 978-1-963874-77-8 (hdcv)
e-ISBN: 978-1-963874-78-5

FIRST EDITION

Disclaimer

The information provided in this book is for informational and inspirational purposes only. It is not intended as, and shall not be understood or construed as, medical, psychological, or professional advice of any kind.

The author is not a licensed medical doctor, psychologist, or healthcare provider. The content herein is based on personal experiences, research, and reflections. It should not be used as a substitute for professional medical advice, diagnosis, or treatment.

Always seek the advice of your physician, mental health professional, or other qualified healthcare provider with any questions you may have regarding a medical condition, mental health concern, or treatment plan. Never disregard professional medical advice or delay seeking it because of something you have read in this book.

The author and publisher disclaim any liability for any direct or indirect loss, harm, or damage that may arise from reliance on the information contained in this book. Your use of the information in this book is solely at your own risk.

If you are experiencing a medical emergency, please call 911 (in the U.S.) or your local emergency number immediately. If you are struggling with your mental health, consider reaching out to a licensed therapist, counselor, or support hotline in your area.

To my family, who love me unconditionally and remind me every day that I am enough.

To the doctors who took the time to listen, understand, and give me the diagnosis that changed the course of my life.

To my basketball coaches who pushed me beyond my comfort zone.

To the teachers and counselors who guided and supported me.

To my circle of friends, who stand by me, push me, and support me through every high and low.

To my Jack and Jill family, who encourage me to be a leader in my community.

And above all, to God, who entrusted me with this mission, equipped me with resilience, and will use my story to change the lives of others. Thank you for trusting me with this journey.

Thank you!

Contents

Introduction

I was eight years old when my **second-grade teacher** pulled my parents aside. She told them I had something she couldn't quite explain. I was afraid of failure. At that age, I didn't know what "fear of failure" meant, but I knew the feeling. It was the knot in my stomach when the teacher called on me. It was the voice in my head that told me to stay quiet, to pass the ball, to play it safe.

That voice followed me everywhere—even onto the basketball court. One night during a big game, the ball ended up in my hands with seconds left on the clock. The gym was loud, the crowd was on its feet, and I had a clear look at the basket. But instead of taking the shot, I passed. I was scared I'd miss. I was scared I'd be the reason we lost. My teammate got off a shot, but it didn't fall. We lost anyway.

Walking off that court, I felt crushed. Not because of the loss, but because I knew I hadn't even given myself a chance. That moment stuck with me. I realized my biggest opponent wasn't the other team. It was fear.

Looking back, I now know that my fear had a name: ADHD. It wasn't just about focus. It was also about confidence. It showed up in classrooms when I stayed quiet, even when I knew the answer. It showed up in friendships when I kept walls up. It showed up in games when I hesitated instead of stepping into the moment.

But I've learned that ADHD doesn't have to be the end of the story. It can be the beginning of growth.

This book is my journey about growing up with undetected ADHD, discovering my voice, and learning to walk with confidence. It's about basketball, family, faith, and resilience. It's about the moments when fear held me back and the lessons that taught me how to push forward. It's about how ADHD is an attitude of "so what" AND my newfound "superpower."

Know that ADHD does not have to be the end of your story. It can be the start of your greatness. I want to show you how faith, focus, and fight can transform what looks like a weakness and turn it into strength. I want you to know the voice that says "you're not enough" is a lie. I've lived with that voice. I've played games with it in my head, sat in classrooms with it, walked through life with it. But I've also learned that God's voice is louder. His voice says you *are* enough.

So here I am, telling my story. A story of a young man chasing his Division I dream with ADHD and refusing to let it stop him.

If you're reading this, it's because some part of you is also chasing something. My prayer is that these pages remind you that you are capable, strong, and not alone. Game on.

CHAPTER 1

The Fear of Failure

I didn't know what it was called back then, but I felt it early. When my second-grade teacher told my parents I had a fear of failure, it sounded like something made up. Like a fancy way to say I was nervous or lazy. But it was real. I froze when things got hard, second-guessed myself, and got quiet when I didn't know the answer. I wasn't bad at school, I just didn't trust myself to be right.

Looking back, it wasn't only fear. It was ADHD hiding in plain sight, and when ADHD goes undiagnosed, it finds ways to make you question yourself, no matter how much talent or potential you have. For me, it showed up in silence.

In second grade, while other kids raised their hands to answer questions or ran to the front of the classroom to show off their work, I held back. I knew the answers sometimes, but my hand stayed glued to the desk. What if I was wrong? What if I embarrassed myself? What if everyone thought I wasn't smart?

My teacher saw it before anyone else. She told my parents **I was afraid to fail.** They didn't know what to make of it. To them, I looked like a bright, capable kid who just needed more confidence. But inside, I was fighting a battle no one could see.

On the basketball court, I did the same thing. I had skill. I could dribble, shoot, and defend, but I didn't take risks. If there was a shot to take, I'd pass. If the game was on the line, I didn't demand the ball. I stayed in the background, convinced someone else was better equipped to shine. I'll never forget the first time a coach said this kid can play, but "he thinks he's cool" or "he doesn't have a motor." It hurt so much to hear that because I was stuck in my own way.

It wasn't that I didn't want to be great. I did. But the fear of missing a shot, the fear of letting my team down, kept me from stepping into the moment. My hesitation was louder than my talent.

At that age, nobody thought about ADHD. I wasn't bouncing off the walls or disrupting class, so I didn't fit the stereotype. Instead, my ADHD wore a different mask: self-doubt, hesitation, and silence. The truth is, ADHD doesn't always look like hyperactivity. Sometimes it looks like the quiet kid in the back who doesn't believe in himself. Neither is good.

Fear is powerful. It tells you stories about yourself that aren't true. It whispers, *"You're not ready. You're not enough. Don't even try. God doesn't love you!"* I grew up in a family that prays. Not having faith meant I wasn't just letting myself down, I was letting God down. There's a scripture that I would read, **Matthew 17:20: *"If you have faith as small as a mustard seed, you can say to this mountain, 'Move from here to there,' and it will move. Nothing will be impossible for you."*** A mustard is so small you can barely see it. I didn't even have that.

For me, fear became a pattern. The less I tried, the less confidence I built. The less confidence I built, the more I doubted myself. It was a cycle that followed me through school, sports, and friendships. Since then, I've learned fear isn't a stop sign. It's a signal. It's the body's way of telling you something matters. Because if it matters, it's worth pushing through.

Parents' Note

"When the teacher told us Jordan had a fear of failure, we didn't get it. We thought, "What do you mean? He's smart, he's kind, he's capable." However, looking back, we can see how often he shied away from opportunities. We wish we had known more about ADHD then. Maybe we would've understood that his silence wasn't laziness—it was a struggle and we would have given him the help, tools, and support he needed."

Student Playbook

- Ask your parents (or a trusted adult) for help. Don't isolate yourself.
- Fear feels real, but it isn't always the truth.
- Trying and failing teaches you more than staying silent.
- Raise your hand even when you're unsure. Confidence grows in action.
- On the court, take one risk per practice: a shot, a drive, a leadership moment.
- Affirm yourself daily that you are great.
- Save your favorite quote or scripture in your notes to refer to when you are down.

Inspiration Spotlight: Michael Phelps

Michael Phelps, the most decorated Olympian of all time, was diagnosed with ADHD at nine years old. Teachers told his mom he'd never focus. Coaches worried he'd never discipline himself. But he found swimming, a place where his restless energy turned into gold medals. His story shows that ADHD doesn't have to hold you back. It can become your superpower if you learn how to use it.

CHAPTER 2

Undiagnosed for Too Long

I magine trying to play basketball, and you are the only one with weights on your ankles. That's what living undiagnosed felt like. I wasn't failing. I got good grades. In fact, most people probably thought I was doing just fine. But what they didn't see was the extra mental capacity, energy, and work it took for me to stay on top.

While my classmates could study for a test in a couple of hours, I'd spend twice as long reviewing the same material to feel halfway ready. While my classmates could read a chapter and remember it, I had to re-read the same page three times because my mind would wander. To the outside world, I looked like a good student. Inside, I was an exhausted teenager, always beating myself up.

Where ADHD really stopped me wasn't in test scores or grades—it was in participation. I rarely raised my hand. I never wanted to lead a group project. I stayed quiet even when I knew the answer. My voice lived in my head, not in the classroom.

I only spoke freely with the same few friends. With them, I felt safe. But outside that circle, I shut down. I couldn't bring myself to be open or vulnerable. While teachers saw me as "shy," or worse, uninterested, the truth was more complicated. ADHD made me second-guess my words before I even spoke them.

Basketball was supposed to be my release. The place where I could be bold. But even on the court, the same silence crippled me. I wouldn't be assertive. I wouldn't demand the ball. I wouldn't take the shot, even when I had it. Not because I couldn't, but because I lacked confidence. It was because I would be on this roller coaster. I would have a great game and feel like I'm finally on my way. Then I would have a major setback and not shoot the ball. It was more than frustrating. It was defeating.

ADHD has a way of turning your strengths into setbacks in the form of questions: *What if I miss? What if I'm not good enough?* I had the skill, but I didn't trust it. Coaches told me to be aggressive. Teammates told me to shoot. But I couldn't shake the doubt.

I learned the hard way that hesitation is the enemy of greatness. If you don't take risks—in the classroom, on the court, or in relationships—you stay stuck. For years, I stayed stuck.

ADHD also affected how I connected with people. I didn't allow myself to be vulnerable. I kept walls up in friendships and relationships because I didn't trust that people would accept me if they saw the full me. The distracted, insecure version who wasn't always confident. It wasn't until later that I understood the truth. ADHD didn't just affect my focus. It impacted how I saw myself and how I let others see me.

The hardest part was the constant questioning: *Am I good enough? Am I smart enough? Am I strong enough to make it?*

ADHD made me doubt myself in every arena of life. It wasn't just about schoolwork. It was about my overall identity. I wasn't lazy, but I felt like I had to work harder than everyone else to prove I belonged.

That's the thing about being undiagnosed. You create your own explanations. For me, the explanation was simple but straightforward: *Maybe I'm just not enough.* It took years to unlearn that lie.

Parents' Note

"We can now admit there were times we thought Jordan just needed to push himself harder. He got good grades, so how could anything be wrong? Looking back, we wish we'd understood that effort doesn't always equal ease. He was fighting battles we didn't recognize or have an answer for."

Student Playbook

- Good grades don't mean you're not struggling.
- ADHD often shows up in confidence, not just focus.
- Prepare one question to ask in class.
- Find your "safe friends," but challenge yourself to speak to others, too.
- Remember: hesitation is the enemy of greatness.
- Download an aspirational podcast you can listen to daily. (E.g., *Athletes' Edge* or *The Daily Motivation*)

Inspiration Spotlight: Simone Biles

Simone Biles, the greatest gymnast in history, has ADHD. When critics tried to shame her for it, she spoke up publicly and said, "Having ADHD and taking medicine for it is nothing to be ashamed of." Her bravery in owning her story is a reminder that your diagnosis isn't a weakness. It's part of your journey.

CHAPTER 3

Science, Signs, and Solutions

For years, I thought my struggles were just mine. I thought I was the only one fighting to focus, the only one who had to work twice as hard to keep up. But ADHD, Attention-Deficit Hyperactivity Disorder, is one of the most common neurodevelopmental conditions in the world. Yet so many people go undiagnosed for years, just like I did.

This chapter isn't solely about my story. It's about the bigger picture of ADHD. What it is, what causes it, how it's diagnosed, and what treatments and resources are out there. If you're a student, parent, coach, or teacher, understanding ADHD is the first step to supporting someone who has it.

ADHD is a brain-based condition that affects how a person pays attention, controls impulses, and regulates energy. Some people think it means being "hyper" or "distracted." But it's more complex. ADHD impacts the brain's executive functioning, the part that helps with planning, organization, self-control, and decision-making.

For some, it shows up as hyperactivity: constant movement, talking, or restlessness. For others, it's inattention: trouble focusing, forgetfulness, or difficulty finishing tasks. For many, it's both.

Scientists believe ADHD is caused by differences in how the brain uses chemicals called neurotransmitters, especially dopamine and norepinephrine.[1] These chemicals play a significant role in focus, motivation, and reward.

Brain imaging studies have shown that people with ADHD often have differences in the size and activity of specific brain regions, like the prefrontal cortex (responsible for decision-making and attention).[2]

---

[1] https://pmc.ncbi.nlm.nih.gov/articles/PMC2626918/

[2] Arnsten AF. The Emerging Neurobiology of Attention Deficit Hyperactivity Disorder: The Key Role of the Prefrontal Association Cortex. J Pediatr. 2009 May 1;154(5):I-S43. doi: 10.1016/j.jpeds.2009.01.018. PMID: 20596295; PMCID: PMC2894421.

The critical thing to know is that ADHD isn't about laziness. It's about wiring. The brain is built differently, and once you understand that, you can learn to work with it instead of against it.

It's also important to understand the role of social media in ADHD, as diagnoses have increased over the past twenty years, especially among children and adolescents. In the U.S., the Centers for Disease Control (CDC) notes that about 10% of children (ages 3–17) have been diagnosed with ADHD as of 2019, compared to ~6–7% in the early 2000s. Among adults, diagnoses are also rising—partly due to better awareness and more people seeking evaluations later in life.

The number of cases of ADHD has risen. It is largely genetic and biological, and the rise of social media has influenced how it is understood and diagnosed. Platforms like TikTok and Instagram expose millions to ADHD-related content, raising awareness and encouraging more people to get evaluated. At the same time, the fast-paced, bite-sized design of social media can amplify attention challenges, making symptoms feel stronger in those who already have ADHD and creating ADHD-like behaviors in others. Experts emphasize that social media does not cause ADHD, but it has contributed to increased diagnoses by both intensifying symptoms and normalizing conversations about the condition.

When to Get Diagnosed

Here are some common signs to determine when someone should seek an evaluation for ADHD.

- Trouble sustaining attention in school or work
- Struggles with organization and forgetfulness
- Avoiding tasks that require focus
- Constant fidgeting or restlessness
- Acting impulsively without thinking things through
- Struggles with time management
- Persistent self-doubt despite putting in effort

Diagnosis often starts with a conversation with a pediatrician, psychologist, or psychiatrist. It involves interviews, behavior rating scales, and sometimes classroom or work feedback. The earlier someone gets diagnosed, the sooner they can get tools that actually help.[3]

ADHD doesn't look the same for everyone. Most of what doctors, parents, teachers, and the public know about ADHD is skewed because of the long-time focus on boys with the condition. Research shows that boys are more likely to be diagnosed because they often display hyperactive symptoms like running around, blurting out

---

[3] https://www.cdc.gov/adhd/diagnosis

answers, and disrupting class. Girls, on the other hand, are more likely to have inattentive ADHD, which shows up as daydreaming, struggling quietly, and appearing "shy." "A blind spot is that many girls with ADHD work harder or study more to make up for lapses in attention and planning. This "masking" of and compensating for their ADHD symptoms often leads to a delayed diagnosis when compared with boys."[4]

Race plays a role, too. Studies have shown that Black and Latino children are less likely to be diagnosed with ADHD compared to white children, even when they show the same symptoms.[5]

Sometimes cultural bias, stigma, or lack of access to healthcare keep kids from getting the help they need. That's why representation matters. When kids see athletes, leaders, and creators talking openly about ADHD, it breaks down barriers.

There's no cure for ADHD, but there are effective ways to manage it. The main tools are:

1. **Medication** – Stimulants (like Adderall or Ritalin) or non-stimulants can help balance brain

---

[4] https://www.cedars-sinai.org/blog/why-adhd-goes-undetected-in-girls.html

[5] https://jamanetwork.com/journals/jamanetworkopen/fullarticle/2776807

chemicals to improve focus and reduce impulsivity.

2. **Therapy** – Cognitive Behavioral Therapy (CBT) helps people build coping strategies, manage emotions, and reframe negative self-talk.

3. **School and Work Accommodations** – Things like extra test time, organizational support, or seating adjustments can make a significant difference.

4. **Lifestyle Tools** – Exercise, nutrition, sleep, and mindfulness can all support focus and mood.

5. **Support Systems** – Coaches, mentors, family, and teachers who understand ADHD can help students lean into their strengths instead of only focusing on weaknesses.

Books and Resources for ADHD

If you're a parent, coach, or student looking to learn more, here are a few resources:

- *Driven to Distraction* by Dr. Edward Hallowell and Dr. John Ratey (two Harvard-trained psychiatrists who are leading experts on ADHD)
- *The ADHD Advantage* by Dale Archer
- *Smart but Scattered* by Peg Dawson and Richard Guare

- CHADD (Children and Adults with Attention-Deficit/Hyperactivity Disorder) – www.chadd.org
- ADDitude Magazine – www.additudemag.com

Getting diagnosed doesn't change who you are. It gives you language and tools for what you're experiencing. For me, hearing, "You might have ADHD," heading into my senior year of high school was like someone handing me the rulebook to a game I'd been playing my whole life blindfolded.

If you suspect ADHD in yourself or someone you care about, don't wait. Get professional help! The earlier you know, the sooner you can build confidence, take risks, and stop questioning your worth.

Parents' Note

"When Jordan was little, we thought ADHD meant being wild or uncontrollable. We didn't understand that it could look like silence, hesitation, or fear. If we had known, we would have pushed for answers sooner. Parents, trust your instincts. If something feels off, advocate for your child." And don't be afraid of the diagnosis!

Student Playbook

- If you struggle in silence, speak up. You're not broken. You might just need tools. ASK FOR HELP!

- A diagnosis isn't the end of the world. It's the beginning of understanding. Control your outcome.

- Try one resource at a time: a book, a podcast, or a conversation with a doctor.

- Remember, ADHD brains are wired for creativity, passion, and resilience. Lean into your strengths.

- Ask your school about the support programs available.

- **Do not** be afraid of being stigmatized.

Inspiration Spotlight: Dr. Ned Hallowell

Dr. Edward (Ned) Hallowell, a Harvard-trained psychiatrist, is one of the world's leading voices on ADHD. He not only studies it, but he also lives with it. His work has shown millions of people that ADHD isn't just a challenge. It can also be a gift, fueling creativity, innovation, and drive.

CHAPTER 4

Finally Getting the Answer

I still remember sitting in that office as if it were yesterday. Heading into my senior year, I had big dreams and a mind that never seemed to keep up. I had learned how to fake focus, how to nod like I understood, how to stay late studying so I could scrape together the grades that came easier to others. But I was tired, and enough was enough.

I was sitting in the kitchen with my close family friends. We were talking about senior year and how it was a defining year. My friend's mom said, "I tested my son for ADHD and he is now getting help. He is doing so much better in school and sports." It was like the whole world stopped. My mom looked at me and then at her friend and said, "What did you just say?"

That casual conversation changed my life and trajectory. It was definitely a God moment because we had never thought about ADHD. My friend and I were so much alike and had the same struggles. I can't thank Ms. Mel and Jeremiah enough for their transparency and honesty.

After that conversation, we made an appointment to get tested. When the results came back, my doctor sat me down and said, "Jordan, you have ADHD."

At first, I didn't know how to feel. Relieved? Embarrassed? Angry? All of it hit me at once. But the more he explained, the more I felt something I hadn't in years. Hope.

It wasn't that I couldn't focus because I was lazy. It wasn't that I doubted myself because I was weak. I had ADHD. A real, medical condition. A way my brain was wired. For the first time, I had language for what I'd been fighting all along. I shared the news with my school counselor. She was very empathetic. She said, "Jordan, you aren't alone. Many of your classmates also struggle with ADHD." It was the first time I felt like someone saw me. Not the grades, not the missed assignments, not the basketball potential, but *me*.

That conversation in my kitchen changed everything. Until then, my life felt like trying to play basketball with an invisible weight vest. I worked twice as hard in the classroom, but my brain pulled me sideways when I needed to go straight. I could do the work, and I did, but it drained me.

What I couldn't do was raise my hand in class or risk speaking up, even when I was 100% sure I was right. Or take a chance on the basketball court when the play was or wasn't obvious. My fear of failure wasn't about not caring. It was about my brain convincing me I wasn't enough.

A diagnosis doesn't change your talent, your character, or your heart. But it changes your strategy. Before, I thought success meant pretending my struggles weren't real. After my diagnosis, I realized success meant understanding them, managing them, and using the tools that worked. For example:

- **Dedicated academic support and extended test time** became less about extra help and more about leveling the playing field.
- **Medication** wasn't a crutch. It was a lens that helped me see the ball, the classroom, and my own potential more clearly.
- **Therapy** gave me the space to admit how much shame I carried and to start letting it go.

I didn't tell many people at first. Part of me still worried about the stigma. What would my teammates think? What about my coaches? My friends? But slowly, I realized the silence was heavier than the truth. The more I opened up, the more support I found. My school didn't stigmatize me. They gave me the resources to be successful. My coaches didn't look down on me. Instead, they adjusted their approach. My parents didn't criticize me. They finally understood. My friends didn't laugh. They respected me more.

My diagnosis wasn't just about school. It was about basketball, too. For years, I had been afraid to take risks on the court. ADHD had me second-guessing every move, while my teammates played free. After my diagnosis, I realized mistakes weren't proof that I was broken. They were proof that I was growing. I didn't need to be perfect to be great. I needed to be bold. That shift in mindset changed my game. I started shooting more. Talking more. Leading more. For the first time, I wasn't just playing basketball. I was *becoming a player*.

If I could go back and talk to my younger self, I'd say:

- You're not lazy.
- You're not stupid.
- You're not broken.

- You learn differently, and that's okay.

Diagnosis is the end of the old story you may be telling yourself, and the beginning of a new one. And you must say "So what" because now you know that your setback is your setup for success!

Parents' Note

"When we initially found out Jordan had ADHD, our first thought was guilt. We had spent years thinking he was just distracted, or lazy, or not living up to his potential. We wish we had known earlier. Parents— don't assume. Ask questions. Get help. Sometimes the answer is deeper than what you see."

Student Playbook

- Get diagnosed.
- Know that a diagnosis is not a label. It's a tool.
- Share your truth with people you trust. Support grows in the light, not in silence, including counselors, coaches, and trusted friends.
- On the court, in the classroom, and in life, risk is the road to greatness.

- Remember: confidence doesn't come from perfection. It comes from preparation and progress.

Inspiration Spotlight: Will.i.am

Will.i.am's journey proves that ADHD doesn't limit success but can fuel it. By embracing his unique wiring, he became not only a world-class musician but also a designer, entrepreneur, and philanthropist. His story reminds us that confidence isn't about fitting in. It's about standing out.

CHAPTER 5

Treatment & Daily Maintenance

Getting the ADHD diagnosis was step one. The next question was more complicated. *What do I do now?*

ADHD doesn't disappear when you know its name. The diagnosis gave me clarity, but daily life still demanded strategies, adjustments, and real work. I had to learn that managing ADHD wasn't about "fixing" myself, it was about creating systems that helped me succeed. ADHD treatment isn't one-size-fits-all. For me, it became a toolbox. Some tools worked every day. Others I only needed in certain situations. Over time, the tools had to change as I grew. My toolbox included:

- **Medication**: It helped me focus, but also required adjustment. Finding the right type and dose wasn't instant. It took a lot of patience. I also had to learn when to take it.

- **Therapy**: Talking about my struggles with someone who understood gave me freedom I didn't expect. I wasn't "weak" for needing it. I was stronger because I did.

- **School accommodations**: Extra time on tests, note-taking support, and teachers who were aware of my challenges made a huge difference.

- **Routine**: Morning workouts, journaling, and prayer became anchors that helped my day start with focus. ADHD makes routine feel like a moving target. But without structure, my days could easily spiral. I had to figure out daily anchors or small habits that made big differences. Mine included:

- **Reviewing my goals every morning** kept me centered.

- **Breaking assignments into smaller steps** stopped me from procrastinating until midnight.

- **Using reminders and alarms** wasn't "babying myself." It was building a system that respected how my brain worked.

- **Celebrating wins was mandatory to keep me encouraged.**
- **Leaning into my faith and prayer life centered me and gave me peace.**

One of the biggest breakthroughs was realizing that *discipline is freedom.* It was about setting myself free from chaos and not boxing myself in.

Basketball taught me that daily maintenance is about *practice, not perfection.* Nobody gets every play right. Nobody shoots 100%. The goal is to keep showing up, adjusting, and trying again. ADHD management is the same. Some days I nailed my routine. Other days, I fell off. But the key was not giving up. Every reset was a win.

Faith became one of my most powerful daily tools. When I doubted myself, prayer reminded me that my worth wasn't measured by my GPA or stat line. It was grounded in God's purpose for me. Managing ADHD wasn't just medical, it was spiritual. It meant trusting that my struggle wasn't random but part of a bigger story that could inspire others.

Parents' Note

"When Jordan started treatment, I finally saw him breathe. The weight he had carried for years began to lift. Parents: treatment isn't about making your child someone else. It's about helping them become the best version of themselves."

Student Playbook

- Build a toolbox. Don't rely on one strategy alone.
- Routines matter. Keep them simple, repeatable, and flexible.
- Preparation > Progress NOT perfection. Consistency wins the long game. No one is perfect.
- Faith, family, and focus can ground you when ADHD feels overwhelming.

Inspiration Spotlight: Ty Pennington

TV host Ty Pennington (*Extreme Makeover: Home Edition*) has ADHD and often speaks about how structure and creativity helped him thrive. His energy once made him feel "too much" for the world, but he discovered that ADHD didn't block his success. Instead, it gave him the spark that made him unique.

CHAPTER 6

School Accommodations

For years, I thought school was just harder for me because I wasn't smart enough or disciplined enough. Teachers would say, *"Jordan is bright, but he needs to focus more"* or *"Jordan doesn't speak up enough. He's too quiet."*

My parents would ask questions like, *"Why do you forget things we just told you? Why aren't you being a leader in class? Why aren't you speaking up?"* Inside, I wondered why I couldn't get it together because it felt like I was always letting someone down.

When I finally got diagnosed with ADHD, everything shifted. Suddenly, there were names for what I struggled with, and there were tools and accommodations that could actually help. The problem was timing. I spent a decade wondering what was happening before being diagnosed. In second grade, when my teacher first noticed my fear of failure, no one thought about testing me for ADHD. That wasn't part of the conversation. Instead, I just tried harder. And for years, I managed by getting good grades and giving solid effort. But what people didn't see was the cost. I was working twice as long as my classmates just to keep up.

By middle school, I could memorize information for a test, but I couldn't sit still during long lectures. I'd study late into the night, then freeze on timed exams because my brain worked differently with pressure. Reading and writing were excruciating because they required my full attention to understand the text and write about what I had read. Even writing this book took a lot out of me because of the attention to detail needed. If I had been tested and supported earlier, I might have learned strategies before the stress and self-doubt piled up. By the time I got answers, I was already in the final stretch of high school, and it felt like time was running out.

The conversation with Melanie and cousin pushed my parents to get me tested and then meet with the school. To our surprise and delight, they had a whole process and staff in place to help set up accommodations. During my senior year, my school guided me through the evaluation process step by step. By the time it was finished, I was officially set up for success.

What Helped (Even Late)

Once I was diagnosed, accommodations started to change the game. Things like:

- **Extra time on tests.** This gave me breathing room when my brain needed longer to organize answers.
- **Quiet testing environments.** Without constant noise, I could think clearly.
- **Breaking assignments into smaller steps.** Teachers who did this made big projects feel possible.
- **Coaching on organization.** Learning how to use planners, alarms, and systems helped me stay on top of deadlines.

These weren't magic fixes, but they gave me a fighting chance.

Asking for help felt like weakness. I was used to powering through silently and hiding the struggle. To admit I needed "extra" felt like admitting I wasn't enough. But I had to learn that accommodations aren't about lowering the bar, they're about leveling the playing field.

For someone with ADHD, extra time means you finally have the same chance to show what you know.

Too many Black students get overlooked when it comes to ADHD diagnosis and accommodations. Some get labeled "lazy" or "defiant." Others never get tested because schools don't push for it, or parents don't know what signs to look for. By the time help comes, the damage to their confidence is already done.

Parents' Note

"As parents, we thought Jordan just needed to apply himself more. We regret not knowing sooner about ADHD and accommodations. Parents, don't be afraid to advocate. Ask for testing. Push for services. Sometimes, we don't know what doors can open until we knock."

Student Playbook

- **Ask early.** If you struggle to keep up despite effort, push for testing.
- **Accommodations are tools, not excuses.** They help you compete fairly.
- **Own your needs.** It's not a weakness to request support—it's wisdom.
- **Use your voice.** Self-advocacy is one of the most powerful skills you can learn.

- **Build a support village outside of school.**
  Coaches and friends play a crucial role.

Inspiration Spotlight: Richard Branson

Richard Branson, billionaire founder of Virgin Group, struggled with ADHD and dyslexia. School was tough for him, but once he discovered the right supports, he leaned into his creativity and risk-taking. He often says his ADHD gave him the courage to think differently and build businesses others wouldn't have dared to try. His story proves that the right accommodations—and mindset—can unlock potential that might otherwise stay hidden.

CHAPTER 7

Shame and Silence

For most of my life, I kept my ADHD struggles hidden. Not because I wanted to, but because I felt like I had to. Shame was the invisible wall I built around myself.

From the outside, I looked like I was doing fine. I had friends. I was playing basketball. My grades weren't bad. To most people, I seemed "normal." But inside, I was battling thoughts that wouldn't let me rest: *Why can't I focus like everyone else? Why do I choke when I want to speak up? Why do I keep second-guessing myself? Why don't I make new friends easily? Why won't I take control in a game when I know I'm capable?*

Instead of opening up, I stayed silent. Silence felt safer than explaining something I didn't even understand myself.

In class, I rarely raised my hand. I knew the answers, but I'd rather stay quiet than risk being wrong. My ADHD made me question myself constantly, and the idea of being embarrassed in front of everyone kept me on mute.

Teachers would sometimes say, "Jordan, you're so smart, but you don't participate enough." They didn't know the battle happening in my head. I wasn't just shy. I was silencing myself to avoid failure.

Basketball should've been my safe space, but even there, shame followed me. I hesitated to take shots, even when I had open looks. I passed the ball instead of attacking. Coaches would yell, "Be aggressive, Jordan!" But aggression meant risk, and risk meant failure. I stayed quiet on the court, just like in the classroom.

Friendships were easier. I had a small circle of close friends who knew the real me. But outside of that, I built walls. I didn't want to risk vulnerability, rejection, or misunderstanding. When it came to relationships, I stayed guarded. The problem with shame is that it convinces you to hide the very thing you need to talk about. ADHD made me feel different, and instead of asking for help, I tried harder to blend in. But pretending only made things worse. It kept me from getting the support I needed sooner.

The turning point was when I finally admitted to myself and others that I needed help. It started small: telling my mom and dad I was overwhelmed, confiding in a friend about my struggles, admitting to a teacher that I couldn't always keep up. Every time I spoke out, the shame got weaker.

By senior year, after my diagnosis, I realized silence had been my biggest enemy. Once I spoke up, doors opened. I got accommodations, support, encouragement, and opportunities.

Parents' Note

"As parents, we wish we had known earlier that Jordan's quietness wasn't just personality—it was a struggle. If your child is silent about their challenges, lean in. Ask questions. Create safe spaces. Sometimes silence is a sign they're carrying more than they should."

Student Playbook

- **Silence doesn't mean strength.** Speaking up is how you find solutions.
- **Shame is a liar.** It tells you you're alone when you're not.

- **Start small.** Open up to one trusted friend, parent, or teacher.
- **Your voice matters.** Whether in class, on the court, or in life—don't let silence steal your chance to grow.

Inspiration Spotlight: Kevin Love

NBA star Kevin Love went public about his struggles with anxiety and depression. He admitted that silence almost broke him, but once he spoke up, he became a leader and advocate for mental health. His honesty inspired countless athletes to share their own stories. My journey with ADHD reflects the same truth. Silence isolates, but speaking up builds strength.

CHAPTER 8

Confidence Under Pressure

Pressure is supposed to bring out the best in athletes. The shot clock winding down. The teacher calling your name. The last question on a timed test. For most people, these are moments to step up and shine. For me, they often became moments of doubt. ADHD didn't just make me distracted—it attacked my confidence.

From the outside, I had everything going for me: talent on the court, supportive parents, opportunities at a great school. But internally, I carried a constant question: *Am I really good enough?*

It wasn't just about missing a shot or forgetting a homework assignment. It was deeper. ADHD turned small mistakes into proof, in my mind, that I wasn't capable. A turnover in a game made me wonder if I should even play basketball. A wrong answer in class felt like a spotlight exposing me.

Confidence is like oxygen for an athlete—and mine always felt thin. There were countless times in games where I had the ball, the lane was open, and the crowd was waiting. But instead of attacking, my brain raced through every possible outcome. *What if I miss? What if I get blocked? What if Coach yells at me? What if the coach pulls me out of the game?*

That split-second hesitation was all it took for the opportunity to vanish. Teammates got frustrated. Coaches pulled me out of the game. I'd go back to the bench with my head down, replaying the mistake of not missing the shot, but of never taking it.

The same thing happened in class. I'd study hard and know the material, but when the teacher asked a question, my hand stayed glued to my desk. The risk of being wrong outweighed the chance of being right. It took years to understand the mental and emotional burden I was carrying from all the times I magnified the negative voices in my head and silenced my own confidence.

So many answers and perspectives stayed locked inside of me because I didn't believe in myself enough to speak up. ADHD made me second-guess every thought before it even left my mouth. It was my invisible enemy.

What most people don't understand about ADHD is that it's not just about focus. **It's about confidence**. The constant self-correcting, the racing thoughts, the memory slips—they all add up. After years of struggling quietly, you start to believe the lies:

- *I'm not smart enough.*
- *I'm not a leader.*
- *I don't belong here.*
- *Something is wrong with me.*
- *I'm not a good basketball player*
- *I don't deserve friends*

That's the silent battle ADHD creates. Even when you're performing well, your brain whispers it's not enough.

One of my turning points came during a game in my senior year. We were down by two, with less than a minute left. I had the ball and was wide open at the three-point line. For a second, I felt the old hesitation creep in. Then I remembered something my coach had said to me in practice.

"Pressure doesn't create champions, it reveals them. Trust your work."

I squared up and took the shot. Swish! The gym exploded. For the first time, I realized confidence wasn't about *never* being scared. It was about trusting myself enough to push through the fear whenever it shows up.

Faith also played a huge part in shifting my confidence. Scriptures like Philippians 4:13 *("I can do all things through Christ who strengthens me.")* weren't just words. They became anchors in moments of pressure. ADHD told me I wasn't enough, but faith reminded me I was created with purpose.

When I started praying before games and tests, it gave me a sense of perspective. Pressure moments weren't about proving my worth but were opportunities to show the gifts God had given me.

Parents' Note

"We saw Jordan doubt himself so many times, even when he was more than capable. Parents—remind your kids constantly that they are enough. Confidence doesn't grow overnight, but with love, faith, and encouragement, it can take root even in the hardest seasons."

Student Playbook

- **Take the shot.** Hesitation is the enemy of growth.
- **Trust your preparation.** Confidence is built in practice, not in the moment.

- **Redefine pressure.** It's not proof of weakness. It's proof you're ready.
- **Anchor in faith.** Let God's voice be louder than your doubts.
- **Learn from failures.** Failures are the roadmap to success.
- **Celebrate the small wins.**

Inspiration Spotlight: Giannis Antetokounmpo

Giannis Antetokounmpo, one of the NBA's most dominant players, has often spoken about the mental side of basketball and how he had to overcome doubt and fear to reach the top. His mindset reminds me that fear isn't the enemy—it's an opportunity. Every time I called for the ball in pressure situations, I was practicing that same decision: to face fear head-on and let it turn into confidence. For me, and for anyone with ADHD, that courage to step forward becomes the difference-maker.

CHAPTER 9

ADHD & Relationships

The impact of ADHD goes beyond school and sports. It shapes the way you connect with people. For me, relationships were one of the hardest areas to navigate. Not because I didn't want friends or couldn't get along with people. But because ADHD made it harder to trust myself, open up, and stay consistent in the way others needed me to. At times, I felt like I was wearing an invisible mask. I was always trying to look confident, steady, and outgoing, while inside I was battling self-doubt, hesitation, and distraction. That mask cost me friendships, opportunities for leadership, and chances to grow closer to people who could've helped me.

Throughout high school, I stuck close to my small circle of friends. They knew me, they understood me, and I didn't have to explain myself. With them, I could relax. But outside of that circle I felt exposed. ADHD made me self-conscious, so I avoided putting myself in new situations. I worried about saying the wrong thing, zoning out during conversations, or not being the "fun" or "cool" person people expected.

Looking back, my circle was a blessing. It gave me stability, but it also served as a shield. It kept me from practicing vulnerability and leadership in wider groups.

My basketball teammates saw my hesitation and sometimes misinterpreted it as indifference. When I didn't call out plays loudly enough, or when I passed instead of shooting, it looked like I didn't care. In reality, I cared too much and was overthinking.

ADHD can make small moments of hesitation appear as a lack of confidence or even a lack of effort. That misunderstanding followed me in sports, group projects, and friendships. Teammates would say things like, "Jordan, you're too quiet" or "Bro, why didn't you take that shot?" They didn't see the storm in my head.

When it came to deeper relationships with mentors, coaches, and even early dating, ADHD made me guarded. I rarely let people see my vulnerabilities. I thought if I admitted I struggled to focus, my support circle would see me as lazy or not good enough. So, I put walls up. I didn't let myself be fully known, which meant people only saw part of me. That made relationships feel half-built, like a foundation with no house on top. No one wants to give their all if they don't believe the other person is doing the same. One person who helped me break through is Coach Kavon. He became like a big brother to me. During our workouts, I could just be myself. If I wasn't working hard, he would be honest. But more than anything, he was just as invested in my success as I was. The countless hours on and off the court helped me tremendously. I want him to know, and all of you reading, that everyone needs someone like Coach Kavon in their inner circle.

One thing people rarely talk about is the emotional impact of ADHD. For me, it showed up as:

1. **Rejection Sensitivity**: I took every small criticism personally. A teammate rolling his eyes at me could ruin my mood for the rest of practice.

2. **Overthinking**: I replayed conversations endlessly, wondering if I had said the wrong thing.

3. **Withdrawal**: Instead of risking rejection, I pulled back. I kept my circle small and my voice even smaller.

This cycle made building strong, trusting relationships more difficult than it needed to be.

At some point I realized relationships don't require perfection, they require honesty. When I started opening up about my ADHD, even in small ways, people responded with understanding, not judgment.

Telling a teammate, "Sometimes I hesitate because I'm overthinking," made them more patient. Vulnerability became the key to connection.

What also made me more aware is that my mom, dad, and sister are incredible relationship builders. They would be in rooms and speak to strangers so easily. They would talk about how important relationships are to success. They had no idea how this also put pressure on me and deepened feelings of inadequacy.

Lessons I Learned

- **People can't support struggles they don't know about.** Hiding my ADHD only created distance.
- **True friends lean in.** When I shared my diagnosis, my closest friends stepped up, not away.
- **Relationships thrive on consistency, not perfection.** Even small efforts such as showing up, listening, and communicating go a long way.
- **Understanding relationships is crucial to success.** People need people in every aspect of life.

- **Vulnerability was key to connecting with people.**

Parents' Note

"As parents, we sometimes worry more about grades and wins than relationships. But relationships are where kids find confidence. When Jordan started sharing his challenges with friends and coaches, we watched him transform—not just as an athlete, but as a young man."

Student Playbook

- **Find your circle.** A few true friends are better than a crowd of acquaintances.
- **Don't hide your struggles.** Honesty builds trust faster than perfection ever will.
- **Speak up, even if your voice shakes.** Teammates and teachers need to hear you.
- **Remember: rejection isn't always personal.** Sometimes it's about timing, not you.

Inspiration Spotlight: Justin Timberlake

Justin Timberlake, 10 x grammy award winning musician and celebrated actor, has spoken about living with ADHD and OCD, and how the structure of creative outlets and supportive collaborators helped him focus his energy. Rather than letting ADHD isolate him, he leaned on strong working relationships in music and film that allowed him to thrive. His journey shows that the right people around you can turn a challenge into fuel for success. ADHD may create obstacles, but with trust, teamwork, and belief from others, those obstacles can become stepping stones.

CHAPTER 10

Grades and Focus

ADHD is tricky. On paper, I looked like I was doing fine in school. My grades were good enough that teachers didn't flag me as "falling behind." But what no one saw was how hard I had to work just to keep up.

For every A or B I earned, there were late nights, countless rewrites, and hours of grinding to prove to myself I was smart enough. I'd reread chapters over and over, highlight entire pages of textbooks, and still walk into class unsure if I remembered a thing. The difference between me and many classmates wasn't effort but the amount of energy it took. My brain demanded double the work for the same outcome.

From the outside, I was a student who had it together. Teachers praised my work ethic. Classmates assumed I had no problem balancing sports and school. But inside, I felt like I was drowning.

Focusing in class was a daily battle. While the teacher spoke, my mind would drift—sometimes to basketball, sometimes to music, sometimes to nothing at all. I'd snap back to attention only to realize I had missed key instructions. Taking notes became an art of guessing, piecing together fragments, and hoping I'd figure it out later. This left me frustrated. I wasn't failing, but I wasn't excelling the way I wanted to. It felt like running a marathon in sand. I was moving forward, but slower than everyone else.

Good grades didn't always translate to confidence. In fact, sometimes they made my self-doubt worse. People assumed I understood everything because I had a strong GPA, but the truth was, I often felt like an imposter. ADHD filled my head with questions like:

- *What if they find out I don't really "get it" the way others do?*
- *What if I forget the answer when called on in class?*
- *What if I can't keep up in college when the work doubles?*

The growing gap between my grades and my confidence made me hesitant to speak up. I was afraid that saying the wrong thing would expose me. So, while I was physically in class, I wasn't really *present*.

One of the most challenging parts of having ADHD is the inconsistency. Some days, I could laser in on an assignment and knock it out in an hour. Other days, I'd spend three hours staring at the same paragraph. Deadlines helped, but they also fueled anxiety. I worked best under pressure but hated the toll it took. The stress of waiting until the last minute, paired with my perfectionism, made every assignment feel like a battle between panic and performance.

Fortunately, my senior year was a turning point. Once I had a diagnosis, I was finally able to access support at school. My teachers began to understand why I sometimes needed instructions repeated, or why testing accommodations mattered. I remember the beginning of senior year meeting with all of my teachers to level set my diagnosis and have a conversation about the best approach for their class. This simple tactic opened a door of communication and provided me with confidence that my teachers had my back. Those relationships mattered. It also helped to have extended test time because it removed the panic of racing the clock. I found value in quiet testing rooms because fewer distractions meant I could actually hear my own thoughts. I also benefited from one-on-one check-ins and having teachers pull me aside weekly to make sure I understood the material. These weren't special favors. They were the tools I needed to show what I actually knew.

If ADHD taught me anything, it's resilience. I learned to grind harder than most because I had to. It was exhausting, but it built discipline. Still, I had to balance that with grace, understanding that my worth wasn't tied to perfection. My value wasn't only in grades or scores, but in how I kept showing up. That shift took time, but it changed everything.

Parents' Note

"As parents, it's easy to see the grades and assume everything is fine. But what we learned with Jordan is that grades don't always tell the full story. Sometimes they mask the extra weight a child is carrying. Parents— ask questions, look deeper, and listen closely."

Student Playbook

- **Don't let grades define you.** They're a measure of performance, not intelligence or potential.
- **Advocate for yourself.** Accommodations aren't excuses, they're bridges.

- **Build study systems.** Find routines that work for *your* brain, not just what others do.
- **Celebrate the effort.** Wins are found in persistence, not perfection.
- **Activate relationships.** Teachers want to hear from you.

Inspiration Spotlight: Solange Knowles

Singer and creative visionary, Solange, has spoken openly about struggling with attention and focus in school. Though she excelled in music, she often felt disconnected in traditional classrooms. Instead of letting that define her, she leaned into her creative strengths, eventually becoming one of the most respected voices in music and art. Her story shows that "success" doesn't always look like straight A's. It looks like finding and owning your lane.

CHAPTER 11

Testing Anxiety

For a long time, tests felt like the ultimate enemy. I could study for hours, reread chapters, and memorize every note, but the second I sat down and the clock started ticking, my brain froze. It wasn't that I didn't know the material because I did. But ADHD has a way of hijacking your ability to show what you know in the moments that matter most.

Every test felt like a race. While my classmates seemed to glide through the questions, flipping pages and filling in bubbles, I was stuck rereading the same line, trying to block out every distraction. A chair squeaking. Someone tapping a pencil. The sound of footsteps in the hallway.

The little things that other people ignored were landmines for me.

By the time I refocused, precious minutes had already passed. No matter how well I knew the subject, anxiety crept in: *What if I don't finish? What if I fail? What if this test defines me?*

It's a real thing how ADHD and anxiety team up during tests. It wasn't just about knowing the answer. It was about battling time. My thoughts raced faster than my pencil could move. I second-guessed myself, erased answers, circled back, and sometimes ran out of time entirely. The most frustrating part was hearing, "Just slow down and focus." If only it was that easy. Slowing down meant losing time. Speeding up meant making careless mistakes. It was a lose-lose situation. The first time I took a standardized test, I completely bombed. I beat myself up. "Why didn't you study longer?" "How come you can't remember that answer?" "Why are you so slow?"

Everything changed senior year when I finally got diagnosed. Suddenly, what I thought was a personal weakness had a name and solutions. The school explained the accommodations I could use, including:

- Extended time on tests, including the SAT/ACT
- Testing in a quieter environment
- Breaking long exams into smaller chunks

The first time I took a test with extra time, I almost cried with relief. For once, I could read questions twice if I needed to. It was a mental and literal celebration. I could pause, take a breath, and not panic when my brain wandered. It didn't make tests easy, but it made things feel *fair*. But testing anxiety is about more than grades. It's about self-worth. Every time I stumbled on a timed exam, it chipped away at my confidence. I'd think, *if I can't finish this, how will I survive college?* Or *if my brain locks up here, what will happen in a job interview or a big game?*

I had to remind myself that testing is one measure. It doesn't define intelligence. It doesn't define potential. It definitely doesn't define who I am.

A few strategies that helped me were:

- **Chunking the test.** I'd break it into smaller sections and treat each like a mini-quiz.
- **Breathing techniques.** When panic rose, I'd pause for five deep breaths.
- **Anchor questions.** I answered the ones I knew first to build momentum.
- **Self-talk.** Instead of "I'll never finish," I told myself, "One question at a time."
- **Using the extra time allocated.** I took my time and worked through the problems.

These strategies didn't erase the anxiety, but they gave me tools to fight back.

Parents' Note

"As parents, we thought test struggles meant our son wasn't studying hard enough. We had no idea how much invisible pressure ADHD adds. When we saw him finally get the right accommodations, we realized how much he'd been carrying in silence. Parents—advocate for your kids. Don't let anxiety steal their confidence."

Student Playbook

- **Ask about accommodations.** If you think ADHD might be affecting your testing, talk to a counselor or teacher.
- **Prepare for pressure.** Reduce the shock by practicing with timed practice tests.
- **Protect your mindset.** Remind yourself that tests measure performance, not your worth.
- **Celebrate small wins.** Finishing calmer, even if not perfect, is progress.
- **Get proper rest.** You have to rest your body and mind to perform well.
- **Test scores don't define you.** Some people just aren't great test takers even with extra time.

Inspiration Spotlight: Jim Carrey

Jim Carrey, one of the most successful comedians and actors in Hollywood, has ADHD and has spoken openly about how it shaped him. In school, traditional tests and structured classrooms were a struggle. He often felt misunderstood and out of place, but instead of letting those challenges define him, he leaned into creativity, expression, and relentless practice. His story reminds us that a test score doesn't measure creativity, passion, or impact. Success can come in ways no exam can predict.

CHAPTER 12

Sports Saved Me

For as long as I can remember, basketball was my escape. The sound of sneakers on the hardwood, the rhythm of the ball hitting the floor, the cheers of the crowd—it was the one place I felt most alive.

But even on the court, ADHD followed me. When school felt overwhelming, basketball gave me a way to breathe. Practices and games created structure. Coaches told me where to be, what play to run, and how to adjust. For a while, it seemed like the perfect outlet.

Basketball went from being a sport to being a form of therapy. It was where I could burn energy, connect with teammates, and feel like I belonged. While classrooms left me second-guessing myself, the court gave me a sense of purpose.

Still, ADHD didn't magically disappear when I put on my jersey. In fact, it showed up in ways that frustrated me the most. Beyond hesitating and not trusting my instincts, I'd zone out during team meetings, missing important instructions. Coaches saw my talent but also my hesitation. Teammates encouraged me, but we all knew I wasn't playing at my full potential. I was holding myself back because I lacked self-confidence.

Over time, basketball taught me lessons that went beyond wins and losses. I learned resilience because every missed shot was a reminder that failure wasn't the end, but a part of the growth process. I learned risk-taking because great players don't wait for permission to lead. They step into the moment. Basketball helped me develop focus by forcing me to practice staying present, one play at a time. It also taught me leadership. Even when I wasn't the loudest guy on the team, I learned that leadership comes in many forms, including encouraging a teammate, hustling in practice, and showing up consistently. My teammates became my brothers. They pushed me, encouraged me, and sometimes called me out when I shrank back. Basketball gave me a place to belong when classrooms and social circles felt complicated. These lessons permeated every aspect of my life. Sports gave me proof that even with ADHD, I could succeed when I pushed past self-doubt.

I'll never forget one game my junior year. The team needed me to step up, but I found myself freezing under pressure. Instead of taking the open shot, I passed—again. Afterward, my coach pulled me aside and said, "Jordan, you're better than you think you are. But you'll never prove it if you don't take the shot."

That moment hit me. Basketball was about **skill, preparation, and confidence.** If I wanted to reach my potential, I couldn't let ADHD and fear keep me on the sidelines of my own story.

Parents' Note

"As parents, we were grateful for basketball because it gave our son an outlet. It gave him structure when school felt overwhelming, helped him build important relationships, and it showed us glimpses of the confident young man he could become. We'll always be thankful that sports caught him during the years when he could have gotten lost."

Student Playbook

- **Find your outlet.** Whether it's sports, music, or art, give your energy somewhere to go.

- **Take the shot.** Don't let fear of failure hold you back. Growth comes from risk.

- **Lean into your team.** Surround yourself with people who push you forward.

- **Translate lessons.** What you learn on the court (or stage, or field) can fuel success everywhere else.

- **Visualize the shot going in.** If you can see it, you can do it.

Inspiration Spotlight: Allen Iverson

One of the greatest guards in NBA history, Allen Iverson stood just six feet tall in a league of giants. He was often told he was too small, too reckless, and too unpolished to succeed. But Iverson never let doubt define him. He played with fearless confidence, attacking the basket and taking risks others wouldn't. He proved that belief in yourself—not just talent—is what separates the good from the great. His story speaks to every athlete battling hesitation. Greatness comes from daring to take the shot, even when others doubt you.

CHAPTER 13

Decent Player, Distracted Mind

From the outside looking in, it seemed like I had everything figured out. I made varsity as a freshman and even started. My sophomore year was a breakout. I was first team all-league, first team all-county, and secured a spot on the All-North Jersey boys' team. On paper, I looked like a rising star.

But ADHD had a way of shadowing every success. While others saw the trophies, I felt the hesitation. I knew I had the skills, but I didn't always trust them. I'd hold back in games, hesitate to lead in huddles, and question whether I belonged. Talent alone wasn't enough when confidence lagged behind.

When I transferred to a more competitive school, it felt like hitting the reset button. Everything I had built—my reputation, my friendships, my rhythm—was gone. I had to prove myself all over again. Every practice felt like an audition. Every drill carried pressure. My new teammates didn't know me, and I didn't yet know them. That made my ADHD symptoms feel even louder. Doubt crept in again. I was starting all over!

There were plenty of ups and downs. During some games, I felt unstoppable. Other nights, I played small. I carried the fear of failure into every room, and sometimes it showed in the way I played.

Even when we won, and mind you, we went on to win a State Championship, I still wrestled with the same insecurities. It was proof I could push through, but it didn't erase the mental battles happening in my head.

Finally getting diagnosed with ADHD gave me clarity. I wasn't shy or unmotivated. There was a reason for my struggles. That understanding unlocked something in me. I began to play with freedom. I trusted my instincts, found my voice as a leader, and leaned into risk instead of running from it. For the first time, basketball wasn't about proving I belonged but about showing how far I could go.

Lessons Learned

My journey through that transition taught me:

- **Resilience.** You don't know your strength until you're forced to start over.
- **Confidence grows with understanding.** Once I knew what I was fighting, I stopped fighting myself.
- **Transitions are tests.** Changing environments can break you or build you.

Parents' Note

"We were torn about Jordan transferring schools. We wanted him to feel supported, but we also knew this was part of his growth. Watching him adjust, stumble, and then rise was powerful. The State Championship wasn't just a team win—it was proof to him that even when life forces you to start over, you can still shine."

Student Playbook

- **Be open to change.** Starting over doesn't erase your talent, but it can give you a new stage.
- **Understand yourself.** Labels like ADHD aren't limits. Instead, they're keys to unlocking your potential.

- **Trust the process.** Confidence doesn't come all at once. It grows through every rep, every challenge.
- **Pressure creates diamonds.** I had to go through the challenges to grow into the confident player I am today.

Inspiration Spotlight: Steph Curry

Steph Curry's story proves that being overlooked doesn't define you. Considered "too small" and not athletic enough, he wasn't heavily recruited out of high school. Even in college, many doubted his ability to succeed at the next level. But Curry trusted his game, worked relentlessly, and changed the game of basketball with his shooting.

His journey shows what happens when you embrace your strengths instead of running from doubts. Like Steph, I had to learn that confidence wasn't about being perfect. It was about believing I had what it took, even when others questioned it.

CHAPTER 14

The Power of Stepping Up

L ooking back, I realize God had been giving me opportunities to use my voice long before I recognized them as blessings. It wasn't easy, but every time I stepped into those moments, I grew.

The first one came in grade school when I won the spelling bee. I was nervous, my palms were sweaty, but I spoke each letter with courage I didn't know I had.

Then, in seventh grade, I was chosen as a student leader. The following year, I was denied becoming a student leader, but I created a new position as the President of our school's Honor Society. Both roles (and the rejection) pushed me to lead my classmates, speak up in front of my peers, and represent something bigger than myself.

The moment that really stretched me came in eighth grade when I was asked to give a speech at graduation. Standing on that stage, looking out at a sea of faces, I felt so much fear. But I also felt God's hand steadying me. Speaking in front of everyone was far outside of my comfort zone. I didn't want to fail, but I understood these were opportunities to grow into the person I was meant to be.

As a member of Jack and Jill, I often have to speak publicly. The biggest moment was during the national convention during our senior year. We had to speak in front of the Eastern Region graduating class and parents. There were approximately 100 people gathered in Baltimore, Maryland. As I approached the stage, I tried to recall my 30-second speech. My good friend hit the mic before me. As I walked up to the mic, I remembered to take a deep breath and just speak from the heart. "Hi, my name is Jordan Ghee, and I am the blessed son of Tony and Michele Ghee. In the Fall, I will be doing a post-grad year at The Hotchkiss School to pursue my academic and athletic endeavors." I did it! It allowed me to take that moment as I was ending high school into my next phase of my journey.

Another big test came in seventh grade at basketball camp, where I was one of about 400 other players. I signed up for the three-point shooting and free-throw competitions, but the night before, I was so nervous I couldn't eat.

That morning, I arrived an hour early to practice my shot. By the time the competition started, I was locked in. Out of twenty-five shots in the three-point contest, I made twenty and won. Then came the free throws. I sank nineteen out of twenty, missing only the last one, and won again.

I keep both trophies in my bedroom as a reminder that practice and preparation fuel confidence. Fear doesn't disappear, but when you've done the work, you can trust yourself to rise to the moment.

The most memorable breakthrough came in my senior year on a retreat. A facilitator asked me to stand and share something I had never told anyone. Only God knows why the facilitator chose me, but I spoke my truth.

"I have a fear of failure."

He paused, looked at me with deep respect, and said, "Wow. Thank you for sharing that."

Then he began to speak about greatness and how fear and doubt often block us from living fully as who we are meant to be. A few minutes later, he called on me again.

"When are you going to start on your journey to greatness?" he asked.

I swallowed hard, thought about it for a moment, and finally said, "Today." He smiled and said, "Exactly."

Something broke free inside of me that day. The fear that had gripped me for so long didn't disappear overnight, but it loosened. For the first time, I felt the weight lift off my shoulders. I walked away from that retreat not just with clarity, but with freedom. When I got home that day, I shared with my parents what had happened. They knew I had changed and was on a path of self-confidence needed to succeed in life. Not only because I shared with the room, but also because I had the courage to share with them.

Parents' Note

"We watched Jordan wrestle with fear but also step into opportunities that scared him. From the spelling bee to graduation speeches to that unforgettable retreat, his Jack and Jill graduation, every time he spoke up, we saw God shaping him into a leader. His courage inspired us, too."

Student Playbook

- **Be the first to arrive and the last to leave.** Confidence is built through preparation.

- **Speak your truth.** Sharing honestly about your struggles is often the first step toward freedom.
- **Step into fear.** The things that scare you most may be the very things that unlock your potential.
- **Trust God's timing.** The moments that push you outside your comfort zone are often divine opportunities.
- **Take a deep breath.** You've got this.

Inspiration Spotlight: LeBron James

LeBron James has built a career on stepping up in the biggest moments. From entering the NBA as a teenager under the label "The Chosen One" to leading his teams to multiple championships, he has faced enormous expectations and pressure. His success didn't come from shying away—it came from boldly embracing the stage. LeBron's story reminds me that stepping up isn't about waiting until you feel ready. It's about accepting the weight of the moment, trusting your preparation, and leading with confidence, even when the world is watching.

CHAPTER 15

AAU Basketball – Pressure and Growth

Amateur Athletic Union (AAU) basketball is a competitive travel circuit where high school athletes play on club teams outside of their school season. It brings together some of the most talented players across the country and provides exposure to college coaches, recruiters, and scouts. The competition level is higher than most high school leagues because teams often pull together top athletes from multiple schools. For players with college aspirations, AAU is one of the most important stages to test skills, measure growth, and get seen nationally.

For me, AAU basketball was both a challenge and a blessing. The competition level added pressure I had never felt before. Every game felt like an audition—because, in many ways, it was. College coaches lined the sidelines. Every turnover, every missed shot, every mistake felt magnified. But it also gave me the chance to grow in ways I couldn't have imagined.

I credit a lot of my growth to my teammates, who pushed me to elevate my game, and to my coaches, Peter Marston and Nathaniel Robinson. They didn't just teach me basketball skills—they taught me how to lead, how to respond to failure, and how to trust myself. They reminded me that mistakes could be turned into opportunities. They pushed me to be vocal, to step into leadership, and at times even told me point blank: "You're good enough." Those words stuck with me.

The Hoop Group also deserves my gratitude. They gave me a big stage and believed in me when I was still proving myself. Playing in front of college coaches during those summers was nerve-racking, but it was also the platform I needed. It built confidence and gave me a bridge to my post-grad year. The highlights that they amplified allowed coaches to see my performance even if they couldn't make the game. I am eternally grateful.

One of my proudest AAU moments came during a Hoop Group tournament when we faced the #2 ranked team in the league. The game went into overtime, and I knew it was my time to step up. I scored 17 points and added 5 assists, but more than the stats, it was the mentality that mattered. I called for the ball. I wanted the responsibility of putting the team on my shoulders. We pulled out the win, and in that moment, I experienced one of the greatest personal and athletic victories of my life. It was the kind of game that proved to me—and everyone watching—that I belonged on that stage.

Overall, the summer of 2025 was the best basketball I've ever played. Our team earned the #1 ranking in our Hoop Group division, and I played with more confidence than ever before. That foundation will carry me into my post-grad season, fueling me with the confidence I need to play at my highest level yet.

Parents' Note

"As a parent, watching AAU basketball was both thrilling and nerve-racking. The pressure was real, but I could see how it sharpened Jordan. Each game demanded focus, resilience, and maturity. What impressed me most was how he learned to use his voice on the court—not just to direct plays, but to encourage his teammates. That growth in confidence carried into life outside of basketball, too."

Student Playbook: Lessons from AAU

- **Pressure is a Privilege.** The competition is tough because the opportunity is great.

- **Turn Mistakes into Teaching Moments**. Don't let errors define you. Let them refine you.

- **Leadership Isn't About Age.** Use your voice early. Being a leader is about impact, not seniority.

- **Trust Your Preparation.** In high-pressure games, fall back on your training and routine.

- **Play for the Team, Not Just the Scouts.** Coaches notice players who elevate others.

CHAPTER 16

Faith Over Fear

B y the time I reached my junior and senior years, the pressure had gone beyond grades and basketball. It was about meeting *expectations*. Teachers, coaches, family, and even my own inner voice all seemed to demand more.

On the outside, people saw my good grades, awards, and recognition on the basketball court. But on the inside, I carried a constant fear of letting people down. Every test, every game, every decision felt like it had the power to define me.

The hardest part of ADHD isn't always what people can see. It's what happens in silence. The nights I stayed awake, overthinking every mistake. The frustration of knowing the answer in class but not raising my hand because I doubted myself. The moments in games where I hesitated instead of trusting my instincts.

That silent battle followed me everywhere, and it wore me down. But what I didn't know yet was that pressure could also be a teacher if I let it.

Basketball became a mirror for how I handled life. When the game was close and the clock was running out, I could shrink back or step up. At first, I shrank. I passed up shots. I let other players take the big moments. But deep down, I knew I wanted to lead. Slowly, I began to realize that pressure wasn't the enemy. Pressure was proof that people believed in me. Pressure meant opportunity. When I shifted my mindset, I stopped seeing pressure as a burden and began to see it as fuel.

The turning point came when I started leaning more on my faith. I began to pray not for the pressure to go away, but for the strength to handle it.

Scriptures like **Philippians 4:13** reminded me, *"I can do all things through Christ who strengthens me."*

Instead of asking God to take away the weight, I asked Him to make me stronger under it. And slowly, that's what happened.

One small but powerful step I took was painting a chalkboard wall in my room. On it, I wrote down the goals I wanted to achieve both on the court and in the classroom. Every morning, the first thing I saw was those words staring back at me. Every night, I looked at them again before bed. That chalkboard became a reminder that confidence isn't random. It comes from preparation, prayer, and daily commitment. As my faith evolved, so did my confidence. Midway through my senior year, I updated my scripture. During my local chapter's Jack and Jill graduation (different from the larger Eastern Region graduation), I delivered my graduation speech. I shared my ADHD journey and closed with how I added another scripture to my chalkboard, **John 13:7:** *"Jesus replied, 'You do not realize now what I am doing, but later you will understand.'"* I know every challenge is making me stronger and preparing me for my future success. My relationship with God is a clear path from "so what to my superpower!"

Parents' Note

"We could see how the pressure weighed on Jordan, even when he didn't say it out loud. But we also saw him grow stronger each time. Pressure shaped him, even when it hurt. And when he leaned into God, we saw the shift—he wasn't just surviving pressure anymore, he was learning to thrive under it."

Student Playbook

- **Reframe pressure.** Instead of fearing expectations, see them as proof of your potential.
- **Focus on the process.** Success isn't a single moment, but rather it's built from daily habits.
- **Write it down.** Putting your goals where you can see them daily reinforces discipline.
- **Lean on faith.** God doesn't always remove the fire, but He strengthens you to walk through it.
- **Don't carry it alone.** Talk to coaches, teachers, and friends when the pressure feels too heavy.

Inspiration Spotlight: David Robinson

David Robinson, nicknamed *"The Admiral"* because of his service in the U.S. Navy, is a Hall of Fame NBA center who played his entire career with the San Antonio Spurs. Robinson faced immense pressure, not just as a star athlete but as someone balancing military service, education, and professional basketball. He often spoke about how his faith in God guided him through moments of stress and uncertainty. Robinson believed that pressure wasn't meant to crush him. It was meant to refine him. He leaned on preparation, discipline, and prayer to steady himself in big games and big life decisions.

His story is a reminder that greatness isn't built in the absence of pressure but by how you carry yourself under it. Robinson proved that faith and discipline can turn pressure into purpose.

CHAPTER 17

Leading Through the Noise

S enior year was different. Not just because it was my last year of high school, but because, for the first time, I finally understood myself. Getting diagnosed with ADHD wasn't a label. It was a release. Suddenly, the pieces of my story began to make sense. I was claiming my diagnosis as my superpower.

The late nights of frustration, the hesitation to speak up in class, the constant fear of failure, the struggles to assert myself on the basketball court—it wasn't laziness or lack of talent. It was ADHD. Now I had a name for it, and more importantly, a plan to work with it.

Walking into that senior season, I carried the same basketball, the same shoes, and the same skills, but my mindset had shifted. I wasn't hiding anymore. I started playing with freedom. I attacked the rim when I saw an opening. I didn't pass up shots just because I feared missing. Even when I did miss, I didn't let it haunt me like before. Instead, I bounced back.

In the classroom, I raised my hand more often. I asked for help when I needed it. I used the accommodations my school offered: extended time, organizational support, and strategies that helped me channel my focus. For the first time, I wasn't fighting against myself. I was working with myself.

The change was visible to everyone around me. Teachers noticed I was more engaged. Teammates saw me taking charge on the court. Even my close circle of friends could tell I was opening up more, letting myself be seen.

But the biggest change was internal. For the first time, I believed I could do more than survive high school. I could actually thrive. That senior basketball season was the best of my life. Not just because of wins or stats, but because I finally played without the constant voice of doubt in my head.

I learned to see failure differently. A missed shot wasn't the end of the world, merely one moment in a much bigger story. That lesson freed me to play boldly, lead my teammates, and enjoy the game again. I also had a great academic year, ending with a 3.8 GPA. There were no more excuses. I had the tools and confidence to thrive on and off the court. There was no turning back, only stepping into my very bright future.

Parents' Note

"Watching Jordan embrace his diagnosis and step into his confidence was one of our proudest moments. He had spent years questioning himself, but now he was free. He understood his strengths, accepted his challenges, and chose to keep moving forward."

Student Playbook

- **Embrace your diagnosis.** It doesn't define you. It equips you.
- **Use your tools.** Accommodations, routines, and strategies exist for a reason. Don't be afraid to use them.
- **Redefine failure.** Missing a shot, making a mistake, or stumbling doesn't erase your talent. It's part of your growth.
- **Celebrate growth.** Confidence isn't built in one moment. Rather, it's built over time.
- **Lead with confidence.** Once you stop fearing mistakes, you can step into your true potential.

Inspiration Spotlight: Maya Angelou

Maya Angelou, the legendary poet and author, once said, *"You may encounter many defeats, but you must not be defeated."* She faced racism, trauma, and setbacks, but she never allowed them to define her. Instead, she transformed her struggles into art, wisdom, and inspiration for millions.

Her resilience shows us that naming your struggle and accepting it isn't a sign of weakness. It's the beginning of strength. Like Maya Angelou, I learned that my story was about refusing to let fear or failure hold me back from becoming who I was meant to be.

CHAPTER 18

The Power of Routine

After my diagnosis, one of the biggest game-changers wasn't just treatment or accommodations, but routine. I learned that ADHD thrives in chaos, but confidence thrives in structure.

When I built consistent routines, I started to feel more in control. Instead of scrambling to catch up, I was setting the pace. Instead of always reacting, I was finally leading.

Here's what shifted for me:

- **Morning routine.** The chalkboard visuals on my bedroom wall kept me focused and grounded.
- **Study blocks.** Breaking assignments into smaller chunks made schoolwork less overwhelming.

Instead of staring at a huge project, I focused on one step at a time.

- **Basketball prep.** I committed to showing up early, whether it was to get extra shots up, stretch, or mentally prepare. That extra time gave me confidence.

- **Faith practices.** Prayer and journaling became daily anchors. They reminded me that my identity wasn't defined by my performance, but by God's purpose for me.

Routines helped me stay organized and gave me peace. At first, sticking to a routine felt impossible. My natural instincts wanted to drift, procrastinate, or get distracted. But once I saw the results—better grades, stronger practices, calmer mornings—I realized discipline wasn't punishment. It was freedom. Routine turned into momentum, and momentum turned into confidence.

Parents' Note

"We saw how routine gave Jordan balance. Once he built systems that worked for him, he stopped fighting against himself. Structure gave him confidence—and it gave us peace of mind watching him grow into responsibility."

Student Playbook

- **Start small.** Pick one routine (morning, study, or fitness) and master it before adding more.
- **Use visuals.** A chalkboard, planner, or vision board can keep goals in front of you.
- **Be flexible.** Routines aren't about perfection. They're about giving yourself a framework.
- **Connect to purpose.** A routine only works if it's tied to your "why." Link habits to your bigger goals.
- **Trust the process.** Growth comes from showing up daily, not from waiting for motivation.

Inspiration Spotlight: Serena Williams

Serena Williams, one of the greatest athletes of all time, has often spoken about the power of discipline and preparation. Behind every trophy and championship was a routine of early mornings, strict practice sessions, and consistent mental training.

Her faith and dedication to her craft helped her overcome injuries, setbacks, and doubts. Serena showed that routines don't make life boring. Instead, they create the foundation for extraordinary achievement.

CHAPTER 19

Living Up to a Legacy

Having a supportive family is one of the biggest blessings in my life. My family is everything to me. But being surrounded by high achievers also brought a unique kind of pressure. My parents are accomplished. My sister attends Harvard, one of the world's most prestigious universities. From the outside, people see our family and assume success is automatic.

But when you grow up in a family of achievers, it can feel like you're constantly being measured against a standard you're not sure you can meet. It wasn't that my family ever made me feel less than. They loved and encouraged me. The pressure came from within. *Would I*

ever measure up? Could I be the one who didn't succeed?
What if I failed and let everyone down?

I wanted to make my parents proud. I wanted to show my sister that I could shine in my own way. But with ADHD making me question myself constantly, that internal battle was heavier than most people realized.

I often leaned on my personality to carry me through difficult moments. I wasn't always the loudest, but I knew how to connect with people, make them laugh, and build genuine relationships. Still, even with my personality, I sometimes worried it wasn't enough to cover the gaps I felt in school or basketball. That's the thing about pressure. It convinces you that you're always one mistake away from being exposed.

It took me some time to realize that God didn't call me to be a copy of anyone else in my family. My parents have their journey. My sister has hers. I have mine.

The comparison game was a trap. ADHD made me hyper-aware of every shortcoming, but faith helped me remember: God's purpose for me is unique.

When I finally embraced that truth, I started to feel lighter. I could celebrate my family's success without letting it define me. I could focus on my lane, my calling, and my gifts. The plan God has for my unique journey.

I also accepted that my friends and teammates were on their own unique journeys. I watched as they accepted athletic offers and college acceptances. I was confident in my decision to do a post-grad year at the Hotchkiss School. My newfound confidence and trust in God gave me peace that my decision was a great choice.

My Sister, My Sounding Board

One of the greatest blessings in my life has been my best friend and sister, Taylor. She has always been there for me—not just as family, but as someone who listens without judgment and believes in me even when I don't fully believe in myself. Taylor has a gift for reminding me that I am smart, capable, and strong enough to handle whatever comes my way.

What makes her even more special is that, despite her own incredible success as a thriving student at Harvard and the long list of achievements she's already earned, she never holds that over my head. Instead of making me feel like I need to measure up, she has a way of lifting me up. She never makes me feel less than.

Having her as my sounding board has been a true lifesaver. When ADHD made me question myself, Taylor's steady voice reminded me that my challenges don't define me. My effort, faith, and resilience do. She has inspired me not just with her accomplishments but with her humility, kindness, and the way she constantly pushes me to see the best in myself.

I want to thank Taylor for being more than a sister. She has been an inspiration, a motivator, and a reminder that I can achieve anything I set my mind to.

Parents' Note

"We never wanted Jordan to feel like he had to 'live up' to anyone. We only ever wanted him to be himself. But we understand the pressure he felt—especially in a family of achievers. We've watched him find his voice, and we know now he sees that his journey is just as valuable and uniquely his own."

Student Playbook

- **Don't compare lanes.** Your story is yours, not anyone else's.
- **Lean on your strengths.** Personality, kindness, and perseverance matter as much as grades or titles.
- **Redefine success.** Success is about growth, not perfection.
- **Remember God's plan.** Your path is designed specifically for you. Trust it.
- **Trusted Confidants.** Find a select few people you can trust. *(Remember: trust is earned, not given.)*

Inspiration Spotlight: Russell Wilson

NFL quarterback Russell Wilson grew up in a family of high achievers. His father was a lawyer, his brother a baseball player, and his sister a standout athlete. Wilson often talked about the pressure of living up to his family's accomplishments. But he found his strength through faith in God and relentless preparation. Despite being told he was too small to succeed as a quarterback, Wilson leaned into his own gifts and went on to win a Super Bowl. His story is proof that pressure doesn't have to break you. It can push you to find your own greatness.

CHAPTER 20

Writing My Future

When it came time to write my college essay, I knew I couldn't just talk about grades, sports, or achievements. I had to share my truth. My story wasn't perfect, but it was real. And in that honesty, I found freedom.

That essay became one of the most important things I've ever written. It was me finally owning my journey. It was me declaring that ADHD, failure, and doubt would never define me. Instead, my story would be about faith, resilience, and purpose. It was me releasing all the years that I lacked confidence and held onto the fear of failure.

The essay not only opened doors, but it also unlocked over $1.2 million in academic scholarship offers. Even though I didn't accept any of those awards, because I remain committed to playing Division I basketball, I know it was my honesty, courage, and transparency that made the difference. For the first time, I shared who I really was—with confidence.

Failure, Faith, Resilience: My Journey to Self-Love
By Jordan A. Ghee (My College Essay)

When I was in the second grade, my teacher asked to meet with my parents and informed them that I feared failure. I had no idea how those words would impact my life. My fear of failure did not come from trying and falling short. Rather, it arose from an ever-present voice that whispered in my ear, "I am not enough." I was fighting an invisible opponent. I did not know it at the time, but my struggles with lack of confidence, focus, and feeling out of sync with the world had a name: Attention Deficit Hyperactivity Disorder, commonly referred to as "ADHD."

Years later, when I finally received the official diagnosis, it helped me understand the source of my struggles. However, the diagnosis did not bring a sense of relief. Instead, it introduced a new burden—concern that I would be stigmatized. I learned through research that far too many men carry their struggles in silence. Research states that only 26.4% of Black and Hispanic men ages 18 to 44 who experienced daily feelings of anxiety or depression used mental health services, compared with 45.4% of non-Hispanic White men.[6] As a young Black man, I can relate. I did not understand or appreciate what I was feeling, so I tried to hide my anxiety and ignore the challenges of ADHD until I was introduced to therapy. Therapy became a powerful tool in my toolbox to help me navigate life's challenges.

My faith has also strengthened my ability to overcome self-doubt. I have learned to replace the voice of the enemy with another voice—the voice of God, which is far louder than anything the fear of failure can muster. I have learned that the power of trusting God and relying on my faith can help me overcome obstacles and adversity.

Therapy and faith have given me the courage to accept challenges and adversity as simply a part of my unique story, not the defining characteristics of my journey. They also taught me the value of persistence and discipline. Having achieved a 3.9 GPA, I learned to embrace my personal learning style and now view my ability to overcome as a strength. I realize that ADHD has not been an impediment to my growth. Instead, it's made me more determined, resilient, and faithful.

---

[6] National Center for Health Statistics Data Brief No. 206, 2015

Basketball has also provided new opportunities for growth. After my sophomore year, I transferred to Don Bosco Prep, an athletically and academically more challenging school. This was one of the most challenging times of my childhood. I had to adjust to a new environment, make new friends, excel academically, and be a valuable contributor on a new team. In the end, I developed new relationships, maintained academic excellence, made the starting line-up on a nationally ranked basketball team, and won a State Championship. The transition taught me valuable lessons of leadership, teamwork, discipline, resiliency, mental toughness, and the power of community.

From these lessons, I have learned that to whom much is given, much is required. To that end, I have enjoyed mentoring teammates, raising money for charity, and serving as a board member for the local chapter of Jack and Jill of America, Inc. in various capacities, including Sergeant-at-Arms, Protocol Chair, and Parliamentarian.

I look forward to being a high-performing student-athlete in college, one who excels in the classroom and on the basketball court. I envision a future where my personal struggle with ADHD and my triumph over my fear of failure inspire others.

I am Jordan Ghee—a man of faith, resilience, and purpose. I am ready to use my education and experiences, as well as my talents and voice, to make a positive impact in this world.

Parents' Note

"When we read Jordan's essay, we were moved because we saw our son stand fully in his truth. He turned fear into faith, doubt into determination, and struggle into strength. That's what every parent hopes for. He claimed his setbacks as his superpower.

Student Playbook

- **Share your truth.** Your story is your power.
- **Don't be afraid of failure.** It's part of the journey, not the end.
- **Use your voice.** Writing and speaking about your challenges can inspire others.
- **Faith + hard work = opportunity.** Both matter in opening doors.
- **See obstacles as training.** Every challenge builds resilience.

Inspiration Spotlight: Nelson Mandela

Nelson Mandela, one of the greatest leaders of the 20th century, spent twenty-seven years in prison for standing against apartheid in South Africa. When he was released, he could have stayed silent or chosen bitterness. Instead, he chose to share his story with truth, courage, and forgiveness.

Mandela often said, *"Courage is not the absence of fear, it's inspiring others to move beyond it."* His ability to use his voice, even after decades of suffering, changed the course of a nation.

Just like writing my essay gave me freedom and power, Mandela's life reminds us that telling your truth can inspire transformation. Not just for yourself, but for everyone who hears it.

The Hotchkiss Chapter

After graduating high school, I made a decision that surprised some people. I chose to take a post-graduate year at The Hotchkiss School, one of the best academic institutions in the United States. For me, this was about preparing myself for the next level, academically and athletically.

I knew an extra year would give me the chance to sharpen my skills on the basketball court, grow as a student, and further develop as a leader. It wasn't an easy choice, but it was the right one for me.

Hotchkiss represents opportunity. Here, the level of competition is high, the academics are demanding, and the community challenges me to strive for excellence every day. I don't walk onto campus uncertain. I walk onto it equipped with tools I've gained through every experience leading up to this point.

From therapy to faith to the lessons basketball has taught me about confidence and resilience, I know I'm ready to start fresh with a new team in a new environment and prove myself all over again.

Starting over isn't easy. It means new teammates, new friendships, and a new set of expectations. But this time, I don't carry the same fear of failure that weighed me down in the past. Instead, I carry the strength of knowing that I've faced challenges before and grown stronger because of them.

This year is about showing myself that I can thrive anywhere. Hotchkiss is my opportunity to build a stronger foundation for the future, one that will serve me both on the court and in the classroom.

One of the biggest lessons I've learned is that your journey doesn't have to look like anyone else's. Some players go straight to college. Some step away from the game. I chose to do a post-grad year because it felt like the right path for me.

At first, I wondered what others would think. But I realized the only opinion that truly matters is God's. He's the one who opened this door, and if He opened it, I should walk through it with confidence.

It has been a tremendous start to my Hotchkiss era. My coach is amazing. He is encouraging me to be a leader and play to my potential. My advisor is one of the most supportive people I've encountered during my educational journey. She checks in on a regular basis, makes clear expectations, and creates a safe space to be myself, and is helping navigate my path in a new environment. I have also met some new best friends. They are more than teammates. They are true confidants who will be part of my life long after I leave Hotchkiss.

The only thing left is playing Division I college basketball. It's the 80/20 rule. God has answered so many prayers for new relationships, a great school environment, living with self-confidence, and a competitive basketball team (80%). I know that as I continue to work hard and have faith, God will also open the door for me to play D1 basketball (20%). It's so easy to allow the 20% to take up 100% of your energy. I am reminding myself that God has already answered so many prayers and He will not fail me for the last high school act!

Parents' Note

"When Jordan told us he wanted to attend Hotchkiss for a post-graduate year, we knew he was thinking about more than basketball. He was thinking about his future. As his parents, we are beyond proud because he's learned to trust his instincts, listen to God, and create a path that fits his story—not anyone else's."

Student Playbook

- **Don't rush the process.** Sometimes the best step forward is taking time to prepare.
- **Build on your foundation.** Every lesson you've learned before matters now.

- **Step into new roles.** A new environment is the perfect place to grow into leadership.
- **See the long game.** Success is about using today to set yourself up for tomorrow.
- **Don't be afraid to walk your own path.** Your journey doesn't have to look like anyone else's. Confidence comes when you trust the route God has placed before you.

Inspiration Spotlight: Tim Tebow

Tim Tebow, known for his faith and resilience, didn't follow the typical path either. Many doubted him, criticized his style, and told him he didn't fit the mold. But Tebow stayed true to who he was. His faith in God, combined with relentless preparation, allowed him to rise to greatness in both college football and beyond.

His story reminds me that walking your own path with faith and preparation is the true definition of success.

My Story is still being written...

As I look back on this journey, including the battles with focus, the fear of failure, the weight of expectations, and the moments I almost let fear silence me, I can only give glory to God. ADHD didn't define me, but it did refine me. It pushed me to discover my resilience, lean into my faith, and find purpose in what once felt like weakness.

There was a time when I was afraid to take the game-winning shot because I didn't want to let my teammates down. That fear kept me from stepping fully into my moment. But now I know you don't lose when you try. You lose when you let fear keep you from trying at all. God has taught me that failure is not final. It's fuel. Every misstep, every struggle, every doubt has prepared me for the path I'm walking today.

This is my story, but know that your story, with all of its highs and lows, is powerful too. Perhaps you don't fully understand your journey either. But I promise, you will. God already has your path and purpose outlined.

This book isn't just about me. It's about you, too. Whether you're living with ADHD, chasing a dream, or just fighting through the quiet battles of life, know that you have everything you need inside of you to win. Keep your faith strong, your focus sharp, and keep fighting for the life God has called you to live. Here's to making your "So What" your Superpower.

GAME ON!

Closing Prayer

Heavenly Father,

I lift up every person who has read these words. You know their story. You know their struggles. You know their dreams. I pray that something in these pages has reminded them that they are not alone and that you are with them in every step, every stumble, and every victory.

For those battling fear, replace it with faith and courage. For those weighed down by doubt, fill them with clarity and confidence. For those wrestling with ADHD, anxiety, or challenges they can't explain, remind them that Your strength shines brightest in weakness.

Help them to see that failure is not their identity but simply part of their growth journey. Show them that faith, focus, and fight can carry them through any storm. Give them the boldness to take their shot, the resilience to rise after setbacks, and the wisdom to trust your timing.

As Jesus said in John 13:7, "You do not realize now what I am doing, but later you will understand." Help each reader walk in trust, knowing that every moment, difficult or joyful, is shaping them into the person you designed them to be.

Lord, use their story to inspire others, just as you've used mine. Let them walk away from this book not just motivated, but transformed—ready to step into their purpose with confidence, courage, and unwavering faith In Jesus' name, Amen.

Reader's Reflection & Action Guide

This worksheet is designed to help you reflect on your own journey. Take some time to write your thoughts, pray, and commit to small steps forward.

Reflection Questions

What fears have been holding me back?

How has a fear of failure shown up in my story—school, relationships, sports, or work?

Where do I lack self-confidence?

Where in your life have I seen resilience—times I got back up even after setbacks?

Who will I trust about how I am feeling?

What does John 13:7 ('You do not realize now what I am doing, but later you will understand') mean for you right now?

My Faith Playbook for Growth

Faith: One scripture I will lean into is:

Focus: One daily habit I can build to stay present is:

Fight: One bold step I can take this week to push past fear is:

Personal Affirmations

- I am not defined by failure; I am refined by it.
- My story matters because God is writing it.
- I have the courage to take the shot.
- Faith, focus, and fight are my tools for success.

Looking Forward

Who are the people in my life I can lean on for support?

What dream feels too big for me right now?

What legacy do I want my story to leave behind?

ADHD-Centered Podcasts & Where to Listen

1. Journey With Me Through ADHD: A Podcast for Kids

- Best for: Kids & teens, short episodes (5–10 min)
- Apple Podcasts | Spotify

2. ADHD reWired

- Best for: Older teens & young adults, longer episodes (45–90 min)
- Website | Apple Podcasts | Spotify

3. I Have ADHD Podcast

- Best for: Teens/young adults, real-life strategies
- Website | Apple Podcasts | Spotify

4. Taking Control: The ADHD Podcast

- Best for: Productivity, organization, time management
- Website | Apple Podcasts | Spotify

5. ADHD Experts Podcast (ADDitude)
- Best for: Learning from doctors & ADHD experts, Q&A style
- Website | Apple Podcasts | Spotify

6. All Things ADHD (CHADD)
- Best for: General ADHD topics, families & students
- Website | Apple Podcasts | Spotify

7. Translating ADHD
- Best for: Deep dives into ADHD experience & frameworks
- Website | Apple Podcasts | Spotify

8. All Aboard ADHD
- Best for: Tweens, teens, families; approachable ADHD talk
- Website | Apple Podcasts | Spotify